Best Kids' Jokes EVER!

VOLUME 2

Highlights Press
Honesdale, Pennsylvania

Cover Design by Colleen Pidell
Contributing Illustrators: David Coulson, Kelly Kennedy, Pat N. Lewis, Mike Lowery, Rich Powell, Kevin Rechin, Rick Stromoski, Brian Michael Weaver, Pete Whitehead

Published by Highlights Press
815 Church Street
Honesdale, Pennsylvania 18431
ISBN: 978-1-68437-243-0
Manufactured in Dongguan, Guangdong, China
Mfg. 12/2024

First edition
Visit our website at Highlights.com.
10 9 8 7 6

CONTENTS

WHY DID THE CHICKEN CROSS THE ROAD?

Why did the chicken cross the road?

To get to the other side.

Why did the cow cross the road?

To get to the udder side.

Why did the chicken cross the playground?

To get to the other slide.

Why did the turkey cross the road?

To prove she wasn't a chicken.

Why did the pig cross the road?

He thought, "If the chicken can do it, so can I!"

Why did the horse cross the road?

Because it was the chicken's day off.

Why did the chicken cross the road?

Because the road was too long to walk around.

Why did the farmer cross the road?

To bring back his chicken.

What do you call a muddy chicken that crosses the road and crosses back again?

A dirty double crosser.

Why did the gum cross the road?

Because it was stuck to the chicken's foot.

Why did the rooster cross the road?

To cock-a-doodle-doo something.

Why did the rubber chicken cross the road?

She wanted to stretch her legs.

What happened when the elephant crossed the road?

He almost stepped on the chicken!

Jim: Why did the triceratops cross the road?

Bob: I thought the chicken crossed the road.

Jim: Well, why did the chicken cross the road?

Bob: I don't know. Why?

Jim: To get away from the triceratops!

What did the chicken's fortune cookie say?

"Don't cross the road today—it's bad cluck."

Why did the chicken cross the road?

It seemed like an egg-cellent idea.

Why didn't the skeleton cross the road?

It didn't have the guts.

Why did the robot cross the road?

Because the chicken was out of order.

Why did the dinosaur cross the road?

Because the chicken hadn't been discovered yet.

Why did the computer cross the road?

It wanted to get with the program.

Why didn't the ghost cross the road?

It had no body to go with.

Why did the orange stop in the middle of the road?

It ran out of juice.

Why did the chicken cross the book?

To get to the author side.

Why did the germ cross the microscope?

To get to the other slide.

Why did the whale cross the ocean?

To get to the other tide.

Why did the tomato cross the road?

It wanted to ketchup with the chicken.

Why did the chicken cross the road?

To visit her friend.

Knock, knock.

Who's there?

The chicken.

How did the egg cross the frying pan?

It scrambled.

Why did the chicken cross the road?

To boldly go where no chicken had ever gone before.

Why did the chicken stop crossing the road?

She was tired of all the chicken jokes.

JUST JOKING

Mom: John, did you take a shower this morning?

John: Why, is there one missing?

First astronaut: Get ready for launch.

Second astronaut: But I haven't had breakfast yet.

Two frogs were sitting on a lily pad, eating lunch. One said to the other, "Time sure is fun when you're having flies."

Maddie: You know how on a traffic light green means go, yellow means wait, and red means stop?

Elle: Yes.

Maddie: Well, on a banana, green means wait, yellow means go, and red means, "Where did you get that banana?!"

Nurse: Doctor, there's a ghost in the waiting room.

Doctor: Tell him I can't see him.

Mary Poppins ordered cauliflower with cheese and four hard-boiled eggs at her favorite restaurant. As she left the restaurant, she wrote her opinion of the meal in the comment book: "Supercauliflowercheesebuteggswerequite-atrocious."

First snake: Are we poisonous?

Second snake: I don't know. Why?

First snake: I just bit my lip!

Impatient Gardener: This whole row of seeds hasn't sprouted yet!

Patient Gardener: Don't worry. They'll turnip.

First Wall: You know, I can't remember why we're fighting. What came between us?

Second Wall: A room.

A man escaped from prison by digging a hole. After hours of digging, he saw he was in a playground. He leaped in the air and said, "I'm free! I'm free!" A little girl walked up to him and said, "So what? I'm four."

Cary: Did you hear about the two balls of yarn that raced?

Connie: No. Did one of them win?

Cary: They did knot. They wove back and forth, and in the end it was a tie.

One day a bat left to get food and returned with a huge bump on his head.

Bat 1: What happened?

Bat 2: You see that tree over there?

Bat 1: Yes.

Bat 2: Well, I didn't.

First astronaut: If you look down, I think you can see China.

Second astronaut: You've got to be kidding. The next thing I know, you'll tell me I can see knives and forks, too.

A lion was playing checkers with a cheetah. The cheetah skipped across the board and got all the checkers in one move.

"You're a cheetah!" said the lion.

"You're lion!" said the cheetah.

Teacher: Why didn't you finish your homework?

Monster: I was full.

Visitor: You sure grow a lot of peaches around here. What do you do with all of them?

Farmer: We eat what we can and can what we can't.

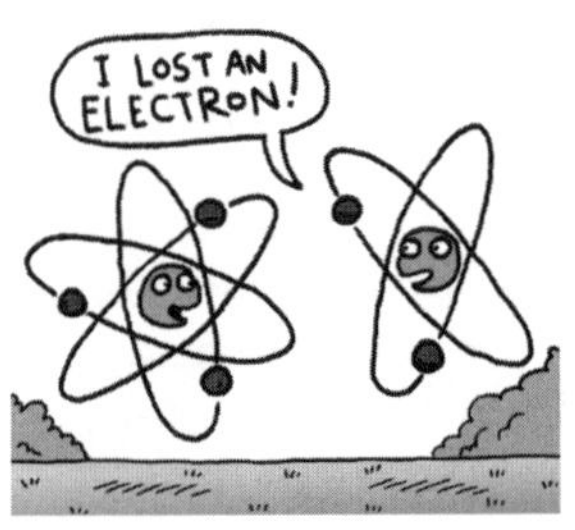

Two atoms were walking down the street.

One said, "I lost an electron!"

"Are you sure?" asked the other.

"I'm positive," said the first.

(At dinner)

Mya: Dad, are bugs good to eat?

Dad: Let's not talk about that at the table.

(After dinner)

Dad: Now, what did you want to ask me?

Mya: Oh, nothing. There was a bug in your soup, but now it's gone.

Brad: Why do bears paint their faces yellow?

Larry: I don't know. Why?

Brad: So they can hide in banana trees.

Larry: Impossible! I've never seen a bear in a banana tree.

Brad: See? It works!

Marielle: I know someone who thinks he's an owl.

Miguel: Who?

Marielle: Make that two people.

Grace: Want to hear a joke about pizza?

Ari: Sure!

Grace: Never mind . . . it's too cheesy.

Ari: Did you hear the joke about the broken pencil?

Grace: No.

Ari: Never mind . . . it's pointless.

Grace: Have you heard the joke about the germ?

Ari: No, what is it?

Grace: Never mind . . . I don't want it to spread.

Ari: Did you hear the joke about the three holes in the ground?

Grace: I haven't.

Ari: Well, well, well.

Grace: Have you heard the joke about the bed?

Ari: No.

Grace: It hasn't been made yet.

Ari: Did you hear the one about the Liberty Bell?

Grace: Yeah, it cracked me up!

Ari: Have you heard the joke about the rocket?

Grace: No.

Ari: It's out of this world!

Sara: Look at that bunch of cows.

Farmer: Not bunch. Herd.

Sara: Heard what?

Farmer: Of cows.

Sara: Sure, I've heard of cows.

Farmer: No! A cow herd.

Sara: So what? I have no secrets from cows!

Girl: How's business?

Tailor: Just sew-sew.

Astronomer: It's looking up.

Farmer: Mine is growing.

Trash collector: It's picking up.

Author: All write.

Elevator operator: Mine has its ups and downs.

Hickory, dickory, dock,
Two mice ran up the clock.
The clock struck one,
And the other one got away.

Matt: What would you do if you were trapped on an iceberg?

Mike: Just chill.

Diner: Do you serve crabs?

Waiter: Yes, we serve anyone.

Fred: Have you heard about the guy whose left side fell off?

Ted: No, how is he doing?

Fred: He's all right now!

First scientist: We have discovered that exercise will help kill germs.

Second scientist: But how in the world are we going to get germs to exercise?

Two muffins are sitting in an oven.

Muffin 1: Does it feel warm in here to you?

Muffin 2: AAH! A talking muffin!

Wacky one-liners

I haven't owned a watch for I don't know how long.

I bought a dog off a blacksmith today. As soon as I got it home, it made a bolt for the door.

There are three kinds of people in this world: those who can do math and those who can't.

A man walked into an antique store and asked, "What's new?"

Today I decided to sell my vacuum. It was just collecting dust.

A book just fell on my head. I only have my shelf to blame.

Don't spell "part" backwards. It's a trap!

I tried to catch some fog yesterday, but I mist.

If you leave alphabet soup on the stove and go out, it could spell disaster.

WHAT'S BLACK AND WHITE AND RED ALL OVER?

What's black and white and red all over?

A newspaper.

What's black and white and red all over?

A sunburned penguin.

What's black and white and red all over?

An embarrassed zebra.

What's black and white and red all over?

A chocolate sundae with ketchup on top.

What's black and white and black and white and black and white?

A panda rolling down a hill.

What's black and white and black and white and black and white?

A zebra in a revolving door.

What's black and white and blue?

A zebra with a cold.

What's gray but can turn red?

An embarrassed rhino.

What's black and white and has sixteen wheels?

A skunk wearing roller skates.

What's black and white and blue all over?

A shivering penguin.

What's white and black and blue all over?

A ghost that can't go through walls.

What's big, white, furry, and always points north?

A polar bearing.

WHAT DO YOU CALL A . . . ?

What do you call a lion at the North Pole?

Lost.

What do you call a camel with no hump?

Humphrey.

What do you call a clam that doesn't share?

A selfish shellfish.

What do you call a shoe made out of a banana?

A slipper.

What do you call a bird that stays up north during winter?

A brrrrd.

What do you call a man who shaves twenty times a day?

A barber.

What do you call a sheep with no legs?

A cloud.

What do you call a sleeping prehistoric reptile?

A dinosnore.

What do you call a bear without an ear?

You call it a B.

What do you call a pirate who skips school?

Captain Hooky.

What do you call two spiders that just got married?

Newlywebs.

What do you call a deer with no eyes?

No-eye deer.

What do you call a deer with no eyes and no legs?

Still no-eye deer.

What do you call a male hippopotamus?

A hippopota-mister.

What do you call a bear with no fur?

A bare bear.

What do you call a bear with no teeth?

A gummy bear.

What do you call a messy crustacean?

A slobster.

What do you call a 500-pound gorilla?

Sir.

What do you call two witches who share the same room?

Broommates.

What do you call a dog that has the flu?

A germy shepherd.

What do you call a ladybug's husband?

Lord Bug.

What do you call a pumpkin that thinks it's a comedian?

A joke-o'-lantern.

What do you call the father of an ear of corn?

Popcorn.

What do you call a traveling flea?

An itch-hiker.

What do you call a number that can't keep still?

A roamin' numeral.

What do you call a clean, neat, hardworking, kind, intelligent monster?

A failure.

What do you call a fly with no wings?

A walk.

What do you call two octopuses that look alike?

I-tentacle twins.

What do you call a pig that knows karate?

A pork chop.

What do you call a boomerang that doesn't come back to you?

A bummerang.

What do you call singing in the shower?

A soap opera.

What do you call rotten eggs, rotten fruit, and spoiled milk in a bag?

Grosseries.

What do you call a royal horse?

His Majesteed.

What do you call it when two dinosaurs crash into each other?

A Tyrannosaurus wreck.

What do you call a gorilla wearing earmuffs?

It doesn't matter. He can't hear you.

What do you call a shivering glass of milk?

A milkshake.

What do you call a skeleton that is always telling lies?

A bony phony.

What do you call a snail on a ship?

A snailor.

What do you call a dog who builds doghouses?

A bark-itect.

What do you call an alligator who is wearing a vest?

An investigator.

What do you call a flying skunk?

A smelly-copter.

What do you call cheese that isn't yours?

Nacho cheese.

What do you call a yo-yo without string?

A no-yo.

What do you call a monkey with all his bananas taken away?

Furious George.

What do you call a fish with no eyes?

A fsh.

What do you call an American drawing?

A Yankee doodle.

What do you call a crate full of ducks?

A box of quackers.

What do you call a snowman in Florida?

Water.

What do you call a hairy beast that is lost?

A where-wolf.

What do you call a bird that smells bad?

A foul fowl.

What do you call a truck full of bison?

A buffa-load.

What do you call a group of people playing bendable musical instruments?

A rubber band.

What do you call a near-sighted dinosaur?

Do-you-think-he-saurus?

What do you call a near-sighted dinosaur's dog?

Do-you-think-he-saurus Rex.

ELE-FUNNIES

What do you call an elephant in a phone booth?

Stuck.

How does an elephant climb a tree?

He stands on an acorn and waits for it to grow.

How does an elephant get down from a tree?

He sits on a leaf and waits for the fall.

What time is it when an elephant sits on your fence?

Time to get a new fence.

Why doesn't the elephant use the computer?

It's afraid of the mouse.

Why did the elephant sit on the marshmallow?

Because she didn't want to fall into the cocoa.

What is beautiful, gray, and wears glass slippers?

Cinder-elephant.

What's the best thing to do if an elephant sneezes?

Get out of its way!

Why don't elephants wear army boots?

Because their ballet slippers are far more comfortable.

What are old bowling balls used for?

Marbles for elephants.

What do you call an animal that never takes a bath?

A smelly-phant.

A doctor looks into a patient's ear.

Doctor: I think I see a whole herd of elephants in there!

Patient: Herd of elephants?

Doctor: Of course I've heard of elephants. Haven't you?

How do you know there is an elephant in your refrigerator?

There are footprints in the butter.

How do you know there are two elephants in your fridge?

You can hear them talking.

How do you know there are three elephants in your fridge?

You can't close the door.

How do you catch an elephant?

Hide in a bush and make a noise like a peanut.

What is as big as an elephant, yet weighs nothing?

An elephant's shadow.

Why did the elephant paint her toenails red?

So she could hide in a bowl of cherries.

Why do ducks have webbed feet?

To stomp out forest fires.

Why do elephants have large feet?

To stomp out flaming ducks.

Why are elephants so wrinkled?

Well, did you ever try to iron one?

How do elephants talk to each other?

They call on the ele-phone.

What would you do if an elephant sat in front of you at a movie?

Miss most of the film.

What do elephants do for laughs?

They tell people jokes.

What goes down but never goes up?

An elephant in an elevator.

Why is an elephant big, gray, and wrinkly?

Because if it was small, white, and smooth, it would be a mint.

CRISS-CROSSED CRACKUPS

What do you get when you cross a dog with a frog?

A dog that can lick you from the other side of the road!

What do you get when you cross a bird, a car, and a dog?

A flying carpet.

What do you get when you cross a US president with a shark?

Jaws Washington.

What do you get when you cross a bear with a rain cloud?

A drizzly bear.

What do you get when you cross peanut butter with a buffalo?

You either get peanut butter that roams the range or a buffalo that sticks to the roof of your mouth.

What do you get when you cross a pig with a frog?

A hamphibian.

What do you get when you cross potato plants with squash plants?

Mashed potatoes.

What do you get when you cross a sheep with a honeybee?

Baa humbug!

What do you get when you cross kangaroos with geckos?

Leaping lizards!

What do you get when you cross a caterpillar with a parrot?

A walkie-talkie.

What do you get when you cross a tarantula with a rose?

I'm not sure, but I wouldn't try smelling it!

What do you get when you cross a chicken with a centipede?

Enough drumsticks to feed an army!

What do you get when you cross a cheetah with a sheep?

A polka-dotted sweater.

What do you get when you cross a rabbit with fleas?

A bugs bunny.

What do you get when you cross a science-fiction film with a toad?

Star Warts.

What do you get when you cross a porcupine with a turtle?

A slowpoke.

What do you get when you cross a great white shark with a trumpetfish?

I don't know, but I wouldn't want to play it!

What kind of animal would you get if you crossed a cocker spaniel, a poodle, and a rooster?

An animal that says, "Cocker-poodle-doo."

What do you get when you cross a newborn snake with a basketball?

A bouncing baby boa.

What do you get when you cross poison ivy with a four-leaf clover?

A rash of good luck.

What do you get when you cross a strawberry with a road?

A traffic jam.

What do you get when you cross an angry sheep and an upset cow?

An animal that's in a baaaaaaaad mooooooood.

What do you get when you cross a dinosaur with a football player?

A quarterback no one can tackle.

What do you get when you cross a snake with a frog?

A jump rope.

What do you get when you cross a kangaroo with an elephant?

Great big holes all over Australia.

What do you get when you cross a parrot with a shark?

A bird that talks your ear off.

What do you get when you cross a sheep and a porcupine?

An animal that can knit its own sweaters.

What do you get when you cross a skunk with a bear?

Winnie the P-U.

KNOCK, KNOCK

Knock, knock.

Who's there?

Banana.

Banana who?

Knock, knock.

Who's there?

Banana.

Banana who?

Knock, knock.

Who's there?

Orange.

Orange who?

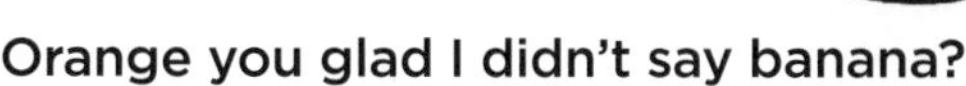

Orange you glad I didn't say banana?

Knock, knock.

Who's there?

Lettuce.

Lettuce who?

Lettuce in. It's cold out here!

Knock, knock.

Who's there?

Amanda.

Amanda who?

Amanda fix the refrigerator is here.

Knock, knock.

Who's there?

Hatch.

Hatch who?

Bless you!

Knock, knock.

Who's there?

Anita.

Anita who?

Anita tissue.

Knock, knock.

Who's there?

Nuisance.

Nuisance who?

What's nuisance yesterday?

Knock, knock.

Who's there?

Olive.

Olive who?

Olive you!

Knock, knock.

Who's there?

Moustache.

Moustache who?

I moustache you a question, but I'll shave it for later.

Will you remember me in a year?

Yes.

Will you remember me in a month?

Yes.

Will you remember me in a week?

Yes.

Knock, knock.

Who's there?

See, you forgot me already.

Knock, knock.

Who's there?

Little old lady.

Little old lady who?

Wow—I didn't know you could yodel!

Knock, knock.

Who's there?

Icing.

Icing who?

Icing in the shower every morning.

Knock, knock.

Who's there?

Justin.

Justin who?

Justin town . . . thought I'd say hi!

Knock, knock.

Who's there?

Dwayne.

Dwayne who?

Dwayne the bathtub—I'm dwowning!

Knock, knock.

Who's there?

Who.

Who who?

I didn't know you spoke Owl!

Knock, knock.

Who's there?

Cereal.

Cereal who?

Cereal pleasure to meet you.

Knock, knock.

Who's there?

Justice.

Justice who?

Justice I thought—no one home.

Knock, knock.

Who's there?

Huron.

Huron who?

Huron my toe. Could you please step off it?

Knock, knock.

Who's there?

Wet.

Wet who?

Wet me in—it's waining!

Knock, knock.

Who's there?

Francis.

Francis who?

Francis in Europe.

Knock, knock.

Who's there?

Jupiter.

Jupiter who?

Jupiter fly in my soup?

Knock, knock.

Who's there?

Icy.

Icy who?

Icy a big polar bear.

Knock, knock.

Who's there?

Rita.

Rita who?

Rita book. It's fun!

Knock, knock.

Who's there?

Adair.

Adair who?

Adair once, but now I'm bald.

Knock, knock.

Who's there?

Adore.

Adore who?

Adore stands between us. Open up!

Knock, knock.

Who's there?

Ice-cream soda.

Ice-cream soda who?

Ice-cream soda whole world will know how silly I am!

Knock, knock.

Who's there?

I'm.

I'm who?

Don't you know who you are?

Knock, knock.

Who's there?

Denise.

Denise who?

Denise are above de ankles.

Knock, knock.

Who's there?

Leaf.

Leaf who?

Leaf me alone.

Knock, knock.

Who's there?

Icon.

Icon who?

Icon tell you another knock-knock joke if you want!

Knock, knock.

Who's there?

Passion.

Passion who?

Passion through and thought I'd say hello.

Knock, knock.

Who's there?

Europe.

Europe who?

Europe to no good, aren't you?

Knock, knock.

Who's there?

Oswald.

Oswald who?

Oswald my bubble gum.

Knock, knock.

Who's there?

Wah.

Wah who?

Well, you don't have to get so excited about it.

Knock, knock.

Who's there?

Cargo.

Cargo who?

Cargo *beep, beep*!

Knock, knock.

Who's there?

Boo.

Boo who?

Don't cry—it's only a joke.

Knock, knock.

Who's there?

Dots.

Dots who?

Dots not important.

Knock, knock.

Who's there?

Lauren.

Lauren who?

Lauren order.

Knock, knock.

Who's there?

Giraffe.

Giraffe who?

Giraffe anything to eat? I'm hungry!

Knock, knock.

Who's there?

Andy.

Andy who?

Andy shoots, Andy scores!

Knock, knock.

Who's there?

Arizona.

Arizona who?

Arizona room for one of us in this town.

Knock, knock.

Who's there?

Waiter.

Waiter who?

Waiter minute while I tie my shoes.

Knock, knock.

Who's there?

T. rex.

T. rex who?

There's a T. rex at your door and you want to know its name?!

Knock, knock.

Who's there?

Sincerely.

Sincerely who?

Sincerely this morning, I've been waiting for you to open this door.

Knock, knock.

Who's there?

Repeat.

Repeat who?

Who, who, who . . .

Knock, knock.

Who's there?

Police.

Police who?

Police stop telling knock-knock jokes.

LOGIC LAUGHS

A man rode his horse to town on Friday. The next day, he rode back on Friday. How is this possible?

The horse's name is Friday.

What starts with T, ends with T, and is full of T?

A teapot.

What word in the English language is pronounced wrong, even by scholars?

Wrong.

Which candle burns longer—a blue candle or a red candle?

Neither. They both burn shorter.

Johnny's mother had three children. The first child was named April. The second child was named May. What was the third child's name?

Johnny.

Why can't you go more than halfway into the woods?

Because then you'd be going out.

What word becomes shorter when you add two letters to it?

Short.

How many men were born in 2006?

No men were born—only babies.

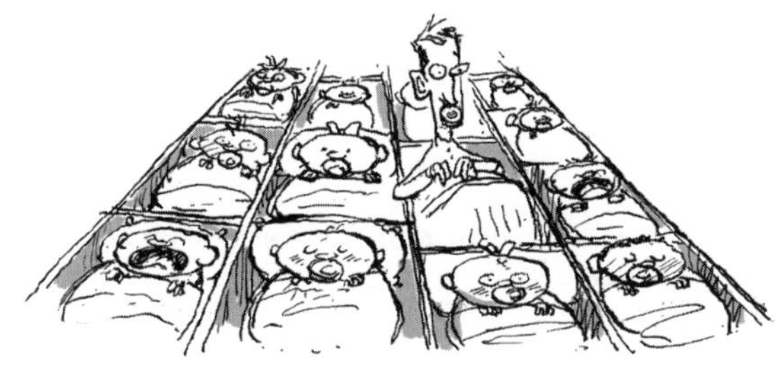

What is so delicate that even saying its name breaks it?

Silence.

How many months have twenty-eight days?

All of them.

What is heavy forward but not backward?

Ton.

Two fathers and two sons order three hamburgers. Each person gets a hamburger. How?

There are only three people: a grandfather, a father, and a son.

Which is faster—hot or cold?

Hot, because you can catch a cold.

What belongs to you but is used mostly by other people?

Your name.

What is easy to get into but hard to get out of?

Trouble.

What goes all the way around the world but never moves an inch?

The equator.

There is an electric train traveling north. Suddenly it turns around and goes south. Which way does the steam go?

It's an electric train—it doesn't have steam.

What goes up and never comes down?

Your age.

What comes down and never goes up?

Rain.

What is harder to catch the faster you run?

Your breath.

You walk into a room with a fireplace, a wood stove, and a kerosene lamp. You have only one match. What do you light first?

The match.

How much dirt is there in a hole that measures two feet by three feet by four feet?

There is no dirt in a hole.

What has a head and tail, but no body?

A coin.

What gets wetter the more it dries?

A towel.

You throw away the outside, cook the inside, eat the outside, and throw away the inside. What is it?

An ear of corn.

What grows when fed but dies when watered?

Fire.

What is three quarters of one million dollars?

Seventy-five cents.

What runs but cannot walk?

Your nose.

What can you serve but not eat?

A tennis ball.

What is dark but made by light?

A shadow.

Before Mount Everest was discovered, what was the highest mountain in the world?

Mount Everest. It just wasn't discovered yet.

What has hands but cannot clap?

A clock.

What kind of bow can't be tied?

A rainbow.

What word does not belong in the following list: meal, deal, steal, real, or heal?

Or.

How do you get out of a house with a table and a mirror but no windows and no doors?

You look in the mirror. You see what you saw. You take the saw and cut the table in half. Two halves make a whole, and you climb through the hole.

What runs but never walks?

Water.

The red house is on the white street, and the blue house is on the red street. Where is the white house?

Washington, DC.

What breaks but never falls, and what falls but never breaks?

Dawn breaks without falling, and night falls without breaking.

What gets lots of answers but no questions?

A doorbell.

What do you find in the middle of nowhere?

The letter H.

The more I appear, the less you see. What am I?

Darkness.

What has cities but no houses, forests but not trees, and water but no fish?

A map.

There are five people in a room. Maya is drawing a picture, Callie is eating an apple, Andrew is playing chess, and Zeke is reading a book. What is the fifth person, Stephanie, doing?

She is playing chess with Andrew.

What can't the strongest man in the world hold for a quarter of an hour?

His breath.

What building has the most stories?

A library.

Is it correct to say "The yolk of the egg is white" or "The yolk of the egg are white"?

Neither is correct—the yolk is yellow.

How can you go without sleep for seven days?

Sleep at night.

What four-letter word can be written forward, backward, or upside down, and can still be read from left to right?

NOON.

What is round on both ends and high in the middle?

Ohio.

What is black when you buy it, red when you use it, and gray when you throw it away?

Coal.

FUNNY FAVORITES

What is a dolphin's favorite TV show?

Whale of Fortune.

What is a golfer's favorite letter?

T.

What is a vampire's favorite animal?

A giraffe.

What is a shark's favorite game?

Swallow the leader.

What is a mouse's favorite game?

Hide-and-squeak.

What is a snowman's favorite game?

Freeze-bee.

What is a tornado's favorite game?

Twister.

What is a dentist's favorite game?

Tooth or dare.

What is a door's favorite kind of joke?

A knock-knock.

What is a tortilla chip's favorite kind of dance?

Salsa.

What is hair's least favorite dance?

The tangle.

What is a detective's favorite dance?

The evi-dance.

What is a banker's favorite dance?

The vaults.

What is a chimpanzee's favorite flavor of ice cream?

Mint-chocolate chimp.

What is a dog's favorite movie?

Jurassic Bark.

What is a cow's favorite movie?

The Sound of Moosic.

What are the solar system's three favorite days of the week?

Saturnday, Sunday, and Moonday.

What is a leopard's favorite day of the week?

Chewsday.

What is a potato's least favorite day of the week?

Fry-day.

What is an English teacher's favorite breakfast?

A synonym roll.

What is a math teacher's favorite dessert?

Pi.

What is a math teacher's favorite kind of candy?

Measure-mints.

What is a teacher's favorite country?

Explanation.

What is a boxer's favorite drink?

Fruit punch.

What is a tree's favorite drink?

Root beer.

What is a llama's favorite drink?

Llama-nade.

What is a llama's favorite food?

Llama beans.

What is a bunny's favorite kind of music?

Hip-hop.

What is a mummy's favorite kind of music?

Wrap.

What is a bumblebee's least favorite musical note?

Bee flat.

What is Tarzan's favorite Christmas carol?

"Jungle Bells."

What is a frog's favorite song?

"Head, Shoulders, Knees, and Toads."

What is a pig's favorite position in baseball?

Snortstop.

What is a ghost's favorite position in soccer?

Ghoulkeeper.

What is a volcano's favorite food?

Magma-roni and cheese.

What is a dinosaur's favorite food?

Macaroni and trees.

What is a knight's favorite food?

Swordfish.

What is a rock star's favorite food?

Jam.

What is a spider's favorite food?

Corn on the cobweb.

What is a dog's favorite kinds of pepper?

Howlapeño.

What are twins' favorite fruit?

Pears.

What is a skeleton's favorite instrument?

A trombone.

What is a trombone's favorite thing on the playground?

The slide.

What is a cat's favorite color?

Purr-ple.

What is a pig's favorite color?

Mahogany.

What is the wind's favorite color?

Blew.

What is a skunk's favorite sandwich?

Peanut butter and smelly.

What is a camera's favorite sandwich?

Cheese.

What is a ghost's favorite sandwich?

Boo-loney.

What is a T. rex's favorite number?

Eight (ate).

What is a statue's favorite dessert?

Marble cake.

What is a rabbit's favorite candy?

Lolli-hops.

What is a goblin's favorite ride at the amusement park?

The roller ghoster.

What is a polar bear's favorite ride at the amusement park?

The polar coaster.

WHAT'S THE DIFFERENCE BETWEEN . . . ?

What's the difference between a fish and a piano?

You can tune a piano, but you can't tuna fish.

What's the difference between a fly and a bird?

A bird can fly, but a fly can't bird!

What's the difference between an injured lion and a cloud?

One pours with rain, and the other roars with pain.

What's the difference between a witch and the letters M-A-K-E-S?

One makes spells, and the others spell "makes."

What's the difference between a dog and a flea?

A dog can have fleas, but a flea can't have dogs.

What's the difference between a hill and a pill?

A hill is hard to get up, and a pill is hard to get down.

What's the difference between a horse and a duck?

One goes quick, and the other goes quack!

What's the difference between a dog and a crocodile?

One's bark is worse than his bite, and one's bite is worse than his bark.

What's the difference between a postage stamp and a girl?

One is a mail fee, and the other is a female.

What's the difference between a comma and a cat?

One means "pause at the end of the clause," and the other means "claws at the end of the paws."

What's the difference between an African rhino and an Indian rhino?

About three thousand miles.

What's the difference between a horse and the weather?

One is reined up, and the other rains down.

Jane: What's the difference between a chimpanzee and a carton of milk?

Shane: I don't know. What?

Jane: Remind me not to send you to the grocery store!

What's the difference between a smart aleck and a man's question?

One is a wise guy, and the other is a guy's why.

What's the difference between a dog and a marine biologist?

One wags a tail, and the other tags a whale.

What's the difference between the law and an ice cube?

One is justice, and the other is just ice.

What's the difference between a coyote and a flea?

One howls on the prairie, and the other prowls on the hairy.

What's the difference between weather and climate?

You can't weather a tree, but you can climate.

What's the difference between a duck and George Washington?

A duck has a bill on its face, and George Washington has his face on a bill.

What's the difference between Santa Claus and a dog?

Santa Claus wears a suit and the dog just pants.

What's the difference between a bunny and a lumberjack?

One chews and hops, and the other hews and chops.

What's the difference between a teacher and a train?

The teacher says, "Spit out your gum," and the train says, "Choo-choo!"

SAY IT AGAIN!

What did the porcupine say to the cactus?

"Are you my mother?"

What did the tie say to the hat?

"You go on ahead and I'll hang around."

What did one volcano say to the other volcano?

"Stop interrupting me!"

What did the buffalo say to his child when he left on a trip?

"Bison."

What did the baby corn say to the mama corn?

"Where's popcorn?"

What did one calculator say to the other?

"You can count on me."

What did the left hand say to the other hand?

"How does it feel to always be right?"

What did one girl firefly say to the other girl firefly?

"You glow, girl!"

What did one elevator say to the other?

"I think I'm coming down with something."

What did the pen say to the pencil?

"So, what's your point?"

What did one worm say to the other worm?

"Where in earth have you been?"

What did the traffic light say to the car?

"Don't look—I'm changing."

What did the green grape say to the purple grape?

"Breathe!"

What did one ocean say to the other?

Nothing. It just waved.

What did the ear of corn say when it was about to be peeled?

"Shucks."

What did George Washington say to his men before they got into the boat?

"Get in the boat, men."

What did one golfer say to the other?

"May the course be with you."

What did one zombie say to the other?

"Get a life."

What did the bubble gum say when it failed its test?

"I blew it."

What did the nine say to the six?

"Why are you standing on your head?"

What did one hurricane say to the other?

"I have my eye on you."

What did the alien say to the garden?

"Take me to your weeder."

What do you say when someone wants your cheese?

"Sorry, but that's nacho cheese."

What do fireflies say to start a race?

"Ready, set, glow!"

What did one snowman say to the other?

"Is it me, or do you smell carrots?"

What did the cheese say when he got his picture taken?

"People!"

What did the police dog say to the speeder?

"Stop in the name of the paw!"

What did summer say to spring?

"Help—I'm going to fall!"

What did the ghost teacher say to the class?

"Look at the board and I will go through it again."

What did the glove say to the baseball?

"Catch you later!"

What did the cow say when it had nothing to eat but a thistle?

"Thistle have to do."

What did the horse say when she finished her hay?

"That's the last straw."

What does a snail riding on a turtle's back say?

"Woo-hoo!"

What did one broom say to the other broom at bedtime?

"Sweep tight."

What did the syrup say to its long-lost friend?

"It's been a waffle long time!"

What did one math book say to the other?

"We've got problems."

What did the guitar say to the musician?

"Quit picking on me!"

What did the zero say to the eight?

"Nice belt."

What did the raindrop say when it fell?

"Oops—I dripped!"

What did one ghost say to the other ghost?

"Do you believe in people?"

What did the hot dog say when it finished the race first?

"I'm the wiener!"

What did one rocket ship say to the other?

"Give me some space!"

What did the horse say when it tripped?

"Oh no! I can't giddy-up!"

What did Benjamin Franklin say when he flew a kite in a lightning storm?

Nothing—he was too shocked.

What did the paper clip say to the magnet?

"You're so attractive!"

What did the hairdresser say to the hot dog?

"Let's put you in a bun."

What did the otter say to the superstar?

"Can I have your otter-graph?"

What does a cookie say when it's excited?

"Chip, chip, hooray!"

What did the beach say when the tide came in?

"Long time no sea."

What did the plus sign say to the minus sign?

"You are so negative."

What did the dog say to the car?

"Hey, you're in my barking spot!"

What did the conductor say to the orchestra?

"We've got a score to settle."

What did the comet say to the sun?

"See you next time around!"

LIGHT BULB JOKES

How many country musicians does it take to change a light bulb?

Five. One to change the bulb, and four to sing about how much they'll miss the old one.

How many superheroes does it take to change a light bulb?

One, and he'll do a super job.

How many carpenters does it take to change a light bulb?

None. That's the electrician's job!

How many drummers does it take to change a light bulb?

One, two . . . one, two, three, four!

How many toucans can change a light bulb?

Two can.

How many chickens does it take to change a light bulb?

None. They're all too busy crossing the road.

How many cavemen does it take to change a light bulb?

What's a light bulb?

One!

How many psychics does it take to change a light bulb?

How many ballerinas does it take to change a light bulb?

Three. One to screw in the bulb and tutu hold the ladder.

How many jugglers does it take to change a light bulb?

One, but he uses at least three bulbs.

How many skunks does it take to change a light bulb?

A phew.

How many seabirds does it take to change a light bulb?

About four or five terns should do the trick.

How many witches does it take to change a light bulb?

Just one, but she changes it into a toad.

How many mystery writers does it take to change a light bulb?

Two. One to screw it in almost all the way, and one to give it a surprise twist at the end.

ROLLICKING RIDDLES

Why was six afraid of seven?

Because 7 8 9.

Where do cows go on vacation?

Moo York.

What is the longest word?

Smiles. There is a mile between the first and last letters.

What's worse than finding a worm in your apple?

Finding half a worm in your apple.

What happens when you tell an egg a great joke?

It cracks up.

What has four legs and flies?

A horse in the summertime.

How many ears did Davy Crockett have?

Three—a left ear, a right ear, and a wild frontier.

How do you have a good party in outer space?

You planet.

What kind of jokes do farmers tell?

Corny ones.

How do you know which end of a worm is its head?

Tickle the middle and see which end laughs.

Where does the general keep his armies?

Up his sleevies.

Who is the leader of the popcorn?

The kernel.

What do you ask a thirsty tyrannosaur?

"Tea, Rex?"

What is the laziest food ever?

Bread—it just loafs around.

What do you do with a blue whale?

Cheer it up.

Why did the golfer wear two pairs of pants?

In case he got a hole in one.

What does a sweet potato wear to bed?

Its yammies.

Why was the scientist's head wet?

Because he had a brainstorm.

When is a door not a door?

When it's ajar.

When is a dog's tail like a farmer's cart?

When it's a-waggin' (wagon).

What happened when the teacher tied all the kids' shoelaces together?

They had a class trip.

How do you make seven even?

Take away the letter S.

What does a ghost put on its bagel?

Scream cheese.

What does a broom do when it's tired?

It goes to sweep.

What kind of bee is hard to understand?

A mumblebee.

What kind of bee trips over its own feet?

A stumblebee.

What kind of bee is bad at football?

A fumblebee.

What do Alexander the Great and Winnie the Pooh have in common?

The same middle name.

Why did the cookie go to the doctor?

It felt crumby.

Why did the banana go to the doctor?

It wasn't peeling well.

What is the definition of a farmer?

Someone who is outstanding in his field.

How much does a pirate pay to get his ears pierced?

A buccaneer.

Why are frogs so happy?

They eat whatever bugs them.

Why can't your nose be twelve inches long?

Because then it would be a foot.

Why does the Statue of Liberty stand in the New York harbor?

Because it can't sit down.

How do you know that carrots are good for your eyes?

Have you ever seen a rabbit wearing glasses?

How do you make a hot dog stand?

Take away its chair.

Why do ballerinas wear tutus?

Three-threes are too big and one-ones are too small.

What is stranger than seeing a catfish?

Seeing a goldfish bowl.

What is more amazing than a talking dog?

A spelling bee.

How do you catch a squirrel?

Climb a tree and act like a nut.

Why couldn't the sailors play cards?

Because the captain was standing on the deck.

What has four legs and says, "Oom, oom"?

A cow walking backwards.

When is a baby good at basketball?

When it's dribbling.

How do you make a strawberry shake?

Take it to a scary movie.

What does the president hang in the White House on the Fourth of July?

The Decorations of Independence.

Who stole the soap from the bathtub?

The robber ducky.

Which side of a chicken has more feathers?

The outside.

How does a polar bear build its house?

Igloos it together.

Why is a flower like the letter A?

Because it's followed by a bee.

How do you catch a unique rabbit?

Unique up on it.

How do you catch a tame rabbit?

The tame way.

When is the best time to go to the dentist?

Tooth-hurty.

Why don't bananas snore?

Because they don't want to wake the rest of the bunch.

What kind of ghost has the best hearing?

The eeriest.

Pretend you are in the jungle and a tiger is chasing you. What do you do?

Stop pretending!

What is the best thing to put in a pie?

Your teeth.

Why is 2+2=5 like your left foot?

It's not right.

Why couldn't the bicycle stand up by itself?

It was two tired.

Why did the farmer throw vegetables on the ground?

He wanted peas on Earth.

What happened to the two bed bugs who met in the mattress?

They got married in the spring.

What would bears be without bees?

Ears.

Why did the clock in the cafeteria always run slow?

Every lunch it went back four seconds.

What dinosaur could jump higher than a house?

All of them—houses can't jump.

Why do birds fly south for the winter?

Because it's too far to walk.

How do you make one disappear?

Add a G, and it's gone.

Why did the traffic light turn red?

You would, too, if you had to change in the middle of the street.

Why did the fly fly?

Because the spider spied her.

What is red and smells like blue paint.

Red paint.

Why can't Dalmatians play hide-and-seek?

They will always be spotted.

How many legs does a horse have if you call its tail a leg?

Four. Calling its tail a leg doesn't make it one!

What do you give to a puppy that has a fever?

Mustard—it's the best thing for a hot dog.

What is the best time to eat a banana?

When the moment is ripe.

If grown-ups have knees, what do children have?

Kid-knees.

How do you make a tissue dance?

Put a little boogey in it.

Why did the triangle jog around the block?

He wanted to get in shape.

What does a nosey pepper do?

It gets jalapeño business.

What do you call a fake noodle?

An impasta.

Which American president wore the largest hat?

The one with the biggest head.

Why is everyone so tired on April 1?

Because they just had a thrity-one-day March.

What did the judge say when a skunk walked into his courtroom?

"Odor in the court!"

What did the judge say about the spoiled milk in the courtroom?

"Odor in the quart!"

Why was there thunder and lightning in the lab?

The scientists were brainstorming.

What's the same about a green apple and a red apple?

They're both red except for the green one.

Why is the letter T like an island?

Because it's in the middle of water.

How tall is a person doing a handstand?

Two feet high.

Where can everyone find money?

In the dictionary.

Why do seagulls fly over the sea?

Because if they flew over the bay, they would be bagels!